ANIMALS IN THE HOUSE:

18 SONNETS

poems by

Sally Cobau

Finishing Line Press
Georgetown, Kentucky

ANIMALS IN THE HOUSE:

18 SONNETS

Copyright © 2025 by Sally Cobau
ISBN 979-8-89990-177-5 First Edition
All rights reserved under International and Pan-American Copyright Conventions. No part of this book may be reproduced in any manner whatsoever without written permission from the publisher, except in the case of brief quotations embodied in critical articles and reviews.

ACKNOWLEDGMENTS

Thanks to the editors who previously published and/or awarded the following poems:

"Airbnb," Semi-finalist in *Humor Contest*, Thank you Jennifer Top.

"Wesel in Winter in the Summer Cottage," Honorable Mention" in *Writer's Digest* Annual Writing Competition. Name to appear in *Writer's Digest* November/December 2024 issue. Thank you Nicole Howard & the team at Writer's Digest.

Although some poems published in the last couple of years are not included here, I would like to give a shout-out to the lovely, hard-working editors of various magazines who accepted and published my poems: Timothy Green of *rattle*; Bill Schulz of *Hole in the Head Review*; Lorette C. Luzajic of *Ekphrastic Review*, and Beate Sigriddaughter of *Writing in a Woman's Voice*. Your encouragement and generosity made all the difference.

Publisher: Leah Huete de Maines
Editor: Christen Kincaid
Cover Art: Artemis Tannett
Author Photo: Artemis Tannett
Cover Design: Elizabeth Maines McCleavy

Order online: www.finishinglinepress.com
also available on amazon.com

Author inquiries and mail orders:
Finishing Line Press
PO Box 1626
Georgetown, Kentucky 40324
USA

Contents

Weasel in Winter in the Summer Cottage 1

Airbnb 2

Mother 3

It Wasn't Fair That You Died or Heather Told Me To Drink The Night My Class For "Troubled Youth" Ended 4

Trying to Find Comfort in the Old Cottage 5

Divine: Summer Instinct 6

Whereupon The Author Wakes Up in the Middle of the Night and Misses Her Children 7

Fruit 8

Sanding The Old Kitchen Table with My Daughter 9

Kids' Games 10

Animals in the House, That Summer 11

Outside Writing 12

Dear Husband 13

Remodeling 14

Upon Finding a Mole in Your Whiskers 15

Bulimia 16

Making Babies 17

How to Write a Sonnet 18

For
Sam   Max   Tess   Fran   George   Dad

Weasel in Winter in the Summer Cottage

We didn't catch the weasel in the house. Run
from him to hymn: "You will outrun your sins."
Did the weasel and snake become friends?
They shared the house by the sea, wretched ones,
slithering up through the old basement's bones
through pipes and floorboards, tacky, murky dirt,
feasting on mice and an array of your shirts
left in the closet, moth-eaten: blue and fair.

I remember summer's sunny daze, honey
for your tea after the drunken party
that settled the score, who wanted more
of this life? So, we swam on a dare from the shore.
It was hard to imagine in summer's helm,
this mess of luxury; the animals' realm.

Airbnb

Dear Owner, a cat happens to be dead
In the well house. We were expecting some
Water, but the pipes were dry. Can you help?
My kid is traumatized and there are ghosts.
You boast of ferns tall as your head, a bed
In a loft that is soft, a kayak stretched
On the plywood dock, short walks to the sea.
None of that is here, I want my money

Back in the good days, Dear Tenant, we left
Doors open, let the ghosts wander where they
Wood is in a pile by the log house. Please
Heir on the side of caution, family's tree.
I had an inkling this would never work.
Take portraits now before you go berserk.

Mother

Do you not see that I am cold, wet, tired?
Out of what is made, I've become a liar.
I was a rugged individualist.
It didn't stop there—borderline Calvinist,
I clasp onto the mountain side, shimmy
my way forth. But, I didn't understand my worth.
With poems in my notebook, I climb mountains,
John Muir's worst gal, I sally fourth

grade there was nothing, just a cracked skull in school
& no one was there to worry at all.
Those who loved me, adored me, the very most
have slipped away; they've all become ghosts.
I remember your gentle touch in my tangled hair.
As the wise writer wrote, *There's no there there.*

It Wasn't Fair That You Died or Heather Told Me to Drink the Night My Class for "Troubled Youth" Ended

It wasn't fair that you died. I would die
instead of you. You asked me what to do
when your mind didn't work anymore. "Just try,"
I said. Think of the dance you always used;
Even when you were dead, they danced for you.
Now I'm with students, too, but I still cry.
Like tonight, I cry for the sad ruse.
How can I explain? Your mind was quite bruised

by the cranium cut, cancer's coil. Drink,
she said as I read these words. Oh, if only it were vulgar,
but they wrote beauty's score. Oh, you didn't blink!
You were brave. There are famous poets, sure.
Whitman with his grass will endure, but what of
Willa with her blunt-cut hair who stutters? Rough,
slumping at the podium, an accident.
I will love her more than this sad event.

Trying to Find Comfort in the Old Cottage

Do you feel the ghosts gathering here?
The tap-tapping of canes, the heavy pie plates?
What about the quivering lights? We drank milk
just to soothe our nerves. You shouldn't arrive late,
but we did, dulled by the night's brilliance, we
thought we had it. The trees were strong, green, alive

as your smile, demure, from years' decree.
Ash in the fireplace, a sort of bribe.
I drank bitter beer in your old, brown cup.
Thought of dulling my pain with medicine.
These pictures look out at me—"Buck up, Pup."
It was Grandpa's wisdom to use Benzedrine.
Thought I would lose myself in old chatter.
Realized I was just a girl in tatters.

Divine: Summer Instinct

I would like to tell you about the moth,
flickering bright on the edge of my mind,
bronzed yellow wings, flapping sap divine.
But it's nothing compared to your round mouth,
plum-ruby, full, licking a cone. Uncouth,
sticky, dripping ice-cream, and the bees, sublime.
I shiver thinking of those sweet, dense times
that became compressed, a swollen moon, a month

or two. It was a graveyard we went to.
Forget insects, moths and mean mosquitoes.
I swallowed them, choked, and wandered through mesquite.
Made food again. From honey. What to do?
The rational? The gluttonous? Take my blood.
Fall to my mother's grave; swarms of bugs above.

Whereupon the Author Wakes Up in the Middle of the Night & Misses Her Children

My naked body and the restless dog.
He nudged the door. I let him out at four
AM, blurry time in the smoky forest
of dreams. I grabbed a drink for my slog.
Where alone in cold hours, I found the old blog
from 2007. I thought then I'd found heaven,
followed the dynamite script: chickens
in the field, homeschooling, arty logs

& I tried my best to compete, replete with
yards of fabric, yards of yarrow, blooming
pastel pink, nostalgia's sorrow. I'm alone,
left with Instagram's Polaroid remorse: kitsch
from projects, cluttered on the sill, spooning
stories, calling the dog back. They're all gone…

Fruit

Today we talked by the peaches, your lush
pyramid a pleasure dome. You seemed drunk
and talked of your Irish roots. I would blush
to hear such stories, but I like apples, shrunk
from the discourse, got saddled by "you're cute."
If only he would concentrate on fruit!

He told me that I told him years ago
that I would love a woman. Oh, I know—
Covid talk! Guilty pleasure in lapses
until the whole swag of fruit collapses
from one woman's graceless hand. She looks at us.
We're talking too much, but I don't want to rush
this gossip. You're king of fruit with a crown,
our world in watermelon seeds be drowned.

Sanding the Old Kitchen Table with my Daughter

At Ace, we got supplies to fix the old wood
table that had graced the nook for years—
cereal with "half a banana," yoked by tears.
But you also remember how Grammie stood
with her boiled hairpins to pick crabs. Should
you shirk your duties, let go of your fears
& spin on her clean floors, your yearning appears
grotesque. Newspapers absorbed the sea crud

from the crab claws. We held our noses, cried,
we couldn't do this anymore, started sanding,
electric hum at night, chips flying, we tried
to do it right. Goggles and brushes, brandishing
our tools to the moon. Then stain and shellac
the ancient pine boards that absorbed sheer cracks.

Kids' Games

*Inspired by "Seasons in the Sun" by Terry Jacks, 1974,
with appreciation for the lines "But the hills that we climbed/Were
just seasons out of time" from "Seasons in the Sun"*

You were always as cute as a button,
while I was never that cute, reddish
hair the color of bark and white teeth. Get on
the makeshift boat before it sinks. Skittish
you. You stink like lobster, like ugly snails.
I would never kiss you! But what of songs?
"Seasons in the Sun"? You jumped on nails.
Remember that? Hooting and hollering. Frogs

and puppy dog tails. Your dad taught you birds
and bees. Happiness to your knees and squeeze
the old door shut. I forget what these verbs
mean exactly: act, slice, kill, love, seize

the day like the mountains we "climbed out of time,"
simply a tragic story; simply a rhyme.

Animals in the House, That Summer

They say the town was infested with mice.
We had our share, too. Kevin found some babes
by his clubs. He was going golfing. Nice
clubs, too. The mice were blind, just like the fable:

"See how they run…" I softened from the overt
fear of the mouse we trapped, those steadfast eyes.
The pets looked askance. Our spastic, black cur
spun on the rug, shed fur, leaped and chased flies—

another problem with the summer. Lies
were told. Promises put on hold. The cats
hunted sparrows and were bold. They left prizes
by the door, then demanded petting and treats.

Mostly we mourned our virile animal who left
dirty socks, scent of Axe and—us—bereft.

Outside Writing

Not quite comedy sketch, but almost so—
I have nestled in green grass with a notebook
when a brown "plop" stains my pages. Let's go!...
back to the beginning. I say "great hook"
is what you need, kids, students, I don't be

live in the water sprinkler's swamped grace,
keep face as you stare in the sun. No course fee;
grade-A meat from the locker. Gradient swagger, lace
your tender thoughts, bet on a long run of nouns:
moose, bear, beer, bow, gun, and long, low shadows
spill across the quad. Sleep in hammocks, rodeo clowns.
Think of hacky sacks, dream girls' backs, windows

into our souls through words, but we want to be heard,
no cowards—find verbs running, hooves of the herd.

Dear Husband

I understand that I was sad when I
should have been happy. Enraged when I should
have been mellow. The cat meows, his eyes
the gold of the sun. If only I could
be good. Gentle. Kind. Run free in the woods
catching birds without song bells around
my neck. A black choker, bracelet, and goods
sparkle on my naked body. I'm bound

by time and place—a figment, a graceful
hound, sleek, grey fur of swimming otter.
If only I could return to the natural.
Days and nights. Days and nights collapse, and blot

out my distinction as I run, walk, fly—
heavy with happiness until I die.

Remodeling

Dizzy from smoke, weed, whatever works,
we were pounding the highway, scrolling phones,
finding bones. Some weird tunes. Then acting like jerks
in the cold Home Depot, a glittering zone.

We were high as we picked out funky tile,
too intricate for the contractor, who
was another guy to flirt with, a rival
but not too bad, the familiar song. I choose

the gleaming bathroom fixture, a silver
head for washing us clean, a can of paint
the color of a bird or Mary's dirndl—
for baptism, new birth. Old lady, I ain't!

But it didn't really change much, the new master bath.
As far as our personalities—they would always clash.

Upon Finding a Mole in Your Whiskers

Dad, did you not tell me about the mole
because you wanted to protect me?
But, of course I asked; that is my role—
dutiful daughter.   Flying to the sea:
coast to coast, we made the most of these trips.
"It was hard," you said. "To shave the stubborn
flesh" that was scraped clean like the waiter's tips.

You and mother. You made me. I was born
with scratchy, black hair, a bad temperament
like your mole: ugliness or beauty mark?
We drove in a white Kia, not quite meant
for these roads, jubilant for the lark.
The brown spot on your face leans towards the sun;
once kissed by your wife, a trembling crumb.

Bulimia

A bulimic's dream—this nice cream and cake,
ready for your adventure, what might you have?
What heady digestive sense? You can't make
me eat carrots or Grape Nuts. I'm a flake. Cave

men and women loved sugar, too, reverse prophesy.
My property… my body was not that good,
not like Marilyn Monroe's, her legacy.
Have you seen her? Sizzling, sweet—better than food.

My aunt cultivated my desire,
bought me silk dresses and a white bunny,
a poster of my idol, black & white fire.
I threw up the crab cakes and found it funny.

Of course, I write these words, as I cry.
Chocolate milk and diet pills. I'm tan. I'll try.

Making Babies

Husband, I miss your big arms, your long sighs-
eleven feet, touching mine. Not touching mine.
What else is there to mend? Let's digress: your eyes
are blue bottles. I bled the red of the wine

we drank, drank one time, times were good, and two,
then three altogether, welded in good weather.
Rough cover, better, pitter-patter. Sew
the black buttons back on. Run towards shelter.

A mix-up of our laughter. I was smart,
and when the tarot card foresaw Death,
I figured it was a metaphor, a chart.
I'm Cancer, you're on the cusp, rangy, stealth…

February. June. Years ago, we clutched
each time, another, on the old bed lucked.

How to Write a Sonnet

Take a can; take the universe and make
them love one another. Undercover.
Of course, of course. The can's shiny splendor.
The universe—black, pitched, it must be fake

as the inky jeweled river. You must slake
your thirst from Coke or seltzer, go under
the way towards shelter, sit and hear thunder
roar its tumble cry; beauty and a rake

come too close. Someone drowned here. Beware woman.
Oh, I'm all right, is what they say, even pain
of childbirth will not keep it taut, sane.
Vowels and consonants, sticking, burgeoning

pushing into the last of the stanza;
the river's rough grass, a full bonanza.

With Thanks

Thank you for the entirely too-much-fun writing group that I'm a part of. Luc, Karin, Shaun, Stephen, and Henrietta, You keep me on my toes and lead me down ridiculous poetry roads.

Thank you to Artemis Tannett for the beautiful cover art.

Also, thanks to the people who are embedded in every word—Fran, Tess, Max, and Sam. You are my muses and my loves. And to my Dad, also my muse and love, whose daily 3:30 calls are the humming songs of these poems, and for my brother, who makes me laugh; who always will. And for my mother, who will always be with us, whose whispered grace is the blood that pumps through my body.

Sally Cobau grew up in Ohio and spent her summers on an island in Maine. In Ohio she played flute in marching band, acted in musicals, and ran through the old barns and cornfields. In Maine, she played with her cousins, gave up shoes for the summer, and picked crabmeat using her grandmother's old hairpins. After graduating from college, she lived in a variety of places including California and Connecticut before going to graduate school in Missoula, Montana. Montana was love at first sight and she became a mountain-river woman, avid hiker, and yoga practitioner. Currently, Sally teaches at a small college in southwestern Montana for traditional students and students enrolled in a military academy. When she's not writing or teaching, she's driving around the state, exploring with her husband and three almost-grownup children.

www.ingramcontent.com/pod-product-compliance
Lightning Source LLC
Chambersburg PA
CBHW022108080426
42734CB00009B/1516